Maybe Your Leg Will Grow Back!

Looking on the Bright Side with Baby Animals

HARPER

NEW YORK • LONDON • TORONTO • SYDNEY

D1361939

Amanda McCall *and Ben Schwartz*

HARPER

All postcard images © Russell Wyse

HarperCollins books may be purchased for educational, business, or sales promotional use. For information please write: Special Markets Department, HarperCollins Publishers, 10 East 53rd Street, New York, NY 10022.

FIRST EDITION

Designed by William Ruoto

ISBN 978-0-06-206507-0

12 13 14 15   OV/RRD   10 9 8 7 6 5 4 3 2

Introduction

Life's tough. No matter how safe you play it, bad things happen, and when they do, it can be hard to look on the bright side . . . until now. *Maybe Your Leg Will Grow Back!* is here to save the day! Did your BFF get roofied? Well, why not let a lovable baby bunny remind her that roofies are high in vitamin C? Sending your nephew to an orphanage? Watch his sad little eyes light up with excitement when a precious puppy explains that orphanages are a great place to meet kids his own age!

As an exclusive bonus, *Maybe Your Leg Will Grow Back!* also features a Do-It-Yourself arts n' crafts section. Turn any horrible document into an adorable document with our DIY baby animal stickers. Cut one out and stick it on anything that needs a little brightening. Your soon-to-be ex-wife will be thanking you for those super cute divorce papers!

And thanks to our new DIY kitten confrontation crown, uncomfortable face-to-face confrontations have never been cuter! Just cut out the crown, place it on your head, and tell your daughter she's adopted. The kitten confrontation crown is guaranteed to turn her frown upside down!

Finally, you can now take care of business . . . with baby animal business cards! Stuck talking to creepy Carl from sales at the office Christmas party? Let a cute lil' kitten tell him you'll never call. He'll be too kitten-smitten to realize he's been rejected.

Remember, no matter how bad the situation, baby animals will help you find the silver lining. When you don't know what to say, say it with baby animals!

Maybe Your Leg
Will Grow Back!

Looking on the Bright Side
with Baby Animals

HARPER

NEW YORK ▪ LONDON ▪ TORONTO ▪ SYDNEY

Maybe Your Leg Will Grow Back!

Looking on the Bright Side with Baby Animals

HARPER

NEW YORK · LONDON · TORONTO · SYDNEY

At least they aren't fourth degree burns!

Maybe Your Leg Will Grow Back!

Looking on the Bright Side with Baby Animals

HARPER

NEW YORK ● LONDON ● TORONTO ● SYDNEY

Maybe Your Leg
Will Grow Back!

Looking on the Bright Side
with Baby Animals

HARPER

NEW YORK ▪ LONDON ▪ TORONTO ▪ SYDNEY

Maybe Your Leg Will Grow Back!

Looking on the Bright Side with Baby Animals

_____

_____

_____

HARPER

NEW YORK • LONDON • TORONTO • SYDNEY

Maybe Your Leg
Will Grow Back!

*Looking on the Bright Side
with Baby Animals*

HARPER

NEW YORK · LONDON · TORONTO · SYDNEY

Maybe Your Leg Will Grow Back!

Looking on the Bright Side with Baby Animals

HARPER

NEW YORK · LONDON · TORONTO · SYDNEY

Maybe Your Leg
Will Grow Back!

Looking on the Bright Side
with Baby Animals

HARPER

NEW YORK · LONDON · TORONTO · SYDNEY

You don't need to finish high school to learn how to smile!

Maybe Your Leg Will Grow Back!

Looking on the Bright Side with Baby Animals

HARPER

NEW YORK · LONDON · TORONTO · SYDNEY

Divorce means you get the bed all to yourself!

Maybe Your Leg Will Grow Back!

Looking on the Bright Side with Baby Animals

_____

_____

_____

HARPER

NEW YORK · LONDON · TORONTO · SYDNEY

Your mug shot will make a perfect profile pic!

Maybe Your Leg Will Grow Back!

Looking on the Bright Side with Baby Animals

HARPER

NEW YORK · LONDON · TORONTO · SYDNEY

If you die before April, you don't have to pay taxes!

Maybe Your Leg
Will Grow Back!

*Looking on the Bright Side
with Baby Animals*

HARPER

NEW YORK · LONDON · TORONTO · SYDNEY

Maybe Your Leg Will Grow Back!

Looking on the Bright Side with Baby Animals

HARPER

NEW YORK · LONDON · TORONTO · SYDNEY

The sluttier your daughter is, the sooner you'll have grandkids!

Maybe Your Leg Will Grow Back!

Looking on the Bright Side with Baby Animals

HARPER

NEW YORK · LONDON · TORONTO · SYDNEY

Maybe Your Leg Will Grow Back!

Looking on the Bright Side with Baby Animals

_____

_____

_____

HARPER

NEW YORK · LONDON · TORONTO · SYDNEY

The odds of getting struck by lightning again are very slim!

Maybe Your Leg
Will Grow Back!

Looking on the Bright Side
with Baby Animals

HARPER

NEW YORK · LONDON · TORONTO · SYDNEY

Guys love widows!

Maybe Your Leg Will Grow Back!

Looking on the Bright Side with Baby Animals

_____

_____

_____

HARPER

NEW YORK ■ LONDON ■ TORONTO ■ SYDNEY

Maybe Your Leg Will Grow Back!

Looking on the Bright Side with Baby Animals

HARPER

NEW YORK • LONDON • TORONTO • SYDNEY

Maybe Your Leg Will Grow Back!

Looking on the Bright Side with Baby Animals

HARPER

NEW YORK · LONDON · TORONTO · SYDNEY

At least you know people aren't dating you for your looks!

Maybe Your Leg Will Grow Back!

Looking on the Bright Side with Baby Animals

_____

_____

_____

HARPER

NEW YORK • LONDON • TORONTO • SYDNEY

Maybe Your Leg Will Grow Back!

Looking on the Bright Side with Baby Animals

HARPER

NEW YORK ₒ LONDON ₒ TORONTO ₒ SYDNEY

At least you got to look right into a solar eclipse!

Maybe Your Leg Will Grow Back!

Looking on the Bright Side with Baby Animals

HARPER

NEW YORK ▪ LONDON ▪ TORONTO ▪ SYDNEY

Maybe Your Leg
Will Grow Back!

*Looking on the Bright Side
with Baby Animals*

_____

_____

_____

HARPER

NEW YORK • LONDON • TORONTO • SYDNEY

Now that you're paralyzed, you don't have to go to the gym!

Maybe Your Leg
Will Grow Back!

*Looking on the Bright Side
with Baby Animals*

HARPER

NEW YORK ・ LONDON ・ TORONTO ・ SYDNEY

Maybe Your Leg
Will Grow Back!

Looking on the Bright Side
with Baby Animals

HARPER

NEW YORK ▪ LONDON ▪ TORONTO ▪ SYDNEY

Maybe your leg will grow back!

Maybe Your Leg
Will Grow Back!

*Looking on the Bright Side
with Baby Animals*

HARPER

NEW YORK · LONDON · TORONTO · SYDNEY

Maybe Your Leg Will Grow Back!

Looking on the Bright Side with Baby Animals

HARPER

NEW YORK · LONDON · TORONTO · SYDNEY

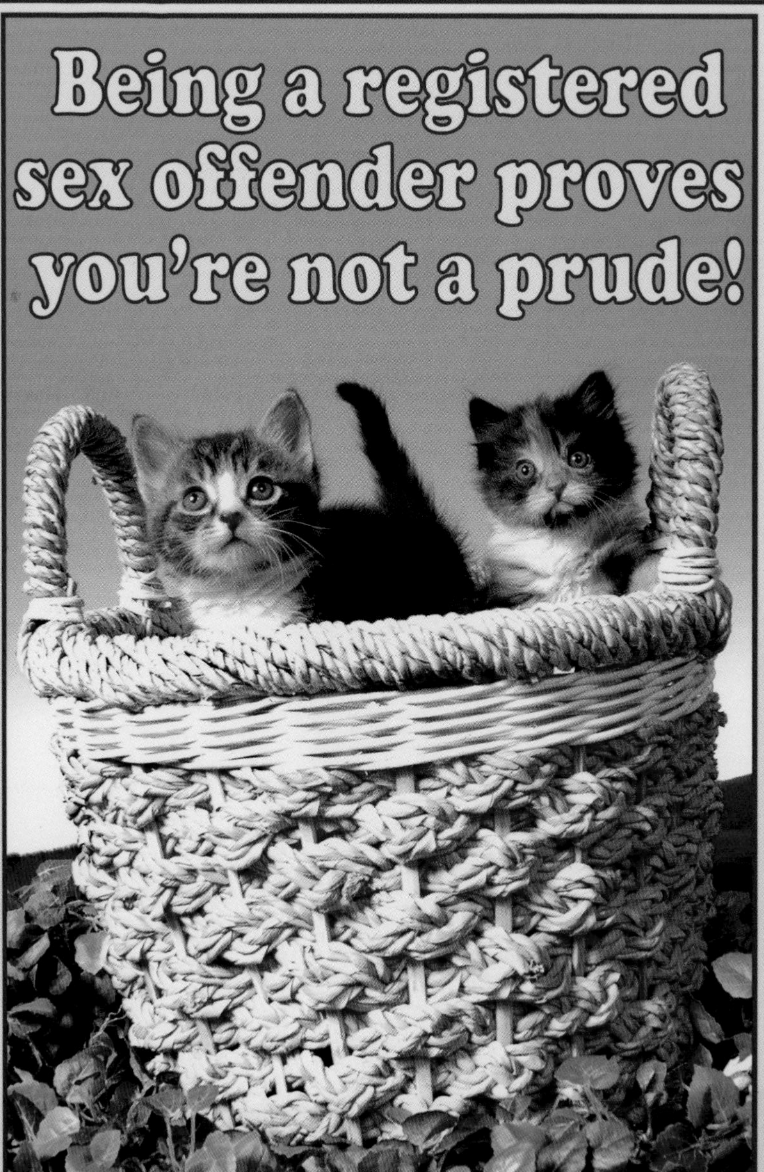
Being a registered
sex offender proves
you're not a prude!

Maybe Your Leg Will Grow Back!

Looking on the Bright Side with Baby Animals

HARPER

NEW YORK · LONDON · TORONTO · SYDNEY

Maybe Your Leg Will Grow Back!

Looking on the Bright Side with Baby Animals

HARPER

NEW YORK · LONDON · TORONTO · SYDNEY

Maybe Your Leg Will Grow Back!

Looking on the Bright Side with Baby Animals

_____

_____

_____

HARPER

NEW YORK · LONDON · TORONTO · SYDNEY

Maybe Your Leg
Will Grow Back!

*Looking on the Bright Side
with Baby Animals*

_____

_____

_____

HARPER

NEW YORK ▪ LONDON ▪ TORONTO ▪ SYDNEY

Maybe Your Leg Will Grow Back!

Looking on the Bright Side with Baby Animals

HARPER

NEW YORK • LONDON • TORONTO • SYDNEY

Maybe Your Leg Will Grow Back!

Looking on the Bright Side with Baby Animals

HARPER

NEW YORK • LONDON • TORONTO • SYDNEY

Your extensive arrest record gives you character!

Maybe Your Leg
Will Grow Back!

*Looking on the Bright Side
with Baby Animals*

HARPER

NEW YORK · LONDON · TORONTO · SYDNEY

Having a rare disease makes you so unique!

Maybe Your Leg
Will Grow Back!

*Looking on the Bright Side
with Baby Animals*

HARPER

NEW YORK · LONDON · TORONTO · SYDNEY

Wetting the bed means you're young at heart!

Maybe Your Leg Will Grow Back!

Looking on the Bright Side with Baby Animals

HARPER

NEW YORK ● LONDON ● TORONTO ● SYDNEY

Maybe Your Leg Will Grow Back!

Looking on the Bright Side with Baby Animals

HARPER

NEW YORK • LONDON • TORONTO • SYDNEY

They say the rice in North Korean prisons is fabulous!

Maybe Your Leg Will Grow Back!

Looking on the Bright Side with Baby Animals

HARPER

NEW YORK · LONDON · TORONTO · SYDNEY

Death might be fun!

Maybe Your Leg
Will Grow Back!

*Looking on the Bright Side
with Baby Animals*

HARPER

NEW YORK · LONDON · TORONTO · SYDNEY

The guy from Boyz II Men has a cane just like that!

Maybe Your Leg Will Grow Back!

Looking on the Bright Side with Baby Animals

HARPER

NEW YORK · LONDON · TORONTO · SYDNEY

Arts n' Crafts

Cut out these baby animals and stick them on anything that needs a little brightening!

Put together this kitten confrontation crown, place on head, and say anything!
Nobody can get mad when your head is covered with adorable kittens!

Leave me alone

I'll never call you

**Cut out these business cards and use them in any uncomfortable
professional or social situation!**

www.sayitwithbabyanimals.com

www.sayitwithbabyanimals.com

Acknowledgments

We would like to thank Jud Laghi, Stephanie Meyers, Russell Wyse, Jenny Arch, Rachel Miller, Jesse Hara, Carrie Kania, Cal Morgan, and our loving friends and families—Bruce, Polly, Floyd, Matthew, Ryan, Mike, Joan, Marni, Jeremy, Brett, and Alexandra.